Meditation and Imagination

Meditation and Imagination

Elleke van Kraalingen

BOOKS

Winchester, UK
Washington, USA

First published by Sixth Books, 2011
Sixth Books is an imprint of John Hunt Publishing Ltd., Laurel House, Station Approach,
Alresford, Hants, SO24 9JH, UK
office1@o-books.net
www.o-books.com

For distributor details and how to order please visit the 'Ordering' section on our website.

Text copyright: Elleke van Kraalingen 2010

ISBN: 978 1 84694 616 5

A CIP catalogue record for this book is available from the British Library.

Design: Stuart Davies

Printed in the UK by CPI Antony Rowe
Printed in the USA by Offset Paperback Mfrs, Inc

We operate a distinctive and ethical publishing philosophy in all
areas of our business, from our global network of authors to
production and worldwide distribution.

CONTENTS

III Imaginations, Reflection, Creative Imagination   **71**
   and Meditation

Word of Thanks

I'm grateful to my inner teachers who have taught me meditation, as well as to Jo and Ajita, who taught me yoga and raja yoga. I am grateful to all teachers over the world whose messages have reached and inspired me in other ways, like the Buddha, Christ, Kahlil Gibran, the Dalai Lama, Thich Nhat Hanh, Michael and Treenie Roads and many others.

In addition, I have learned a lot from all students in my yoga and meditation courses, who have given me feedback by sharing their experiences and asking questions.

Di – without your enthusiasm to edit the manuscript and spend so much time and effort to turn my writing into acceptable English, where would I be? Thank you so much!

Yoram, Tara, Imre and Vivian – you have taught me patience, dedication and flexibility, all of which are necessary to express meditation in daily life. I hope, one day, you'll enjoy this book.

Pieter, my partner in all, my mirror – your support, feedback and resistance is always bringing me further!

Thanks to you all!

Elleke

Preface

A lot of books on meditation have been written before. I know quite a few of them myself. Why, then, another book?

I have often been asked during my courses in meditation, or in my practice as a psychologist, whether I knew of a small, handy-sized book with meditation exercises, which left out the overloading theory: not a book about meditation, but a book with meditations. I did not. And, thus I decided to write one myself.

Meditation is something to do, to experience and, finally, it is a way of being. It is an experience which cannot to be transferred, except by showing someone the way to come to his or her own experience. This book is a practical guide to undertake an explorative journey.

I wish you a lot of joy, insight and inner peace!

With love and respect,

Elleke

Introduction

Around the age of fourteen I encountered spontaneous experiences of altered states of consciousness, accompanied by deep insights. I had not been educated in a religious context and, at the time, I had never heard of the word 'meditation'. But these experiences touched something inside, like memories bubbling up of what I had always known, but could not know.

I received inner teachings and guidance.

To allow these experiences to come more consciously, I sat down, closed my eyes, relaxed, focussed my attention and opened up for whatever would come. And what happened went beyond my imagination. It was a fascinating and exciting process of discovery and growing awareness. Gradually, this focussed relaxation became a daily activity, which brought me a lot of joy, peace, strength and insight, and still does. Soon, I found out that I was better able to relax and concentrate and that my mind was clearer when I did some physical exercises in advance, which I knew from gymnastics. In this way, my yoga developed as a preparation for meditation.

After a year or two, I started to share my experiences with some trusted friends. I got books handed to me and started to read about consciousness, meditation, philosophy and, later, psychology. I went to yoga class to work on a structured base and, a few years later, I started at a teacher training course in yoga and meditation. Out of enthusiasm about the possibilities of the human mind, I started to teach. I have done ever since. Besides teaching, I keep on learning, meditating and playing on a path which is infinite. And that is the idea I want to pass on with this little book: Meditation is not a technique; it is a way of life.

How to Use This Book

It has been said that meditation cannot be learned from a book, but has to be passed on by teacher to student. However, it will be clear from the previous story that I have learned to meditate by myself, without either an external teacher or a book. Later, I started to read about it and went to a course and started to structure and deepen my meditations under the supervision of a teacher. My viewpoint is that meditation is a natural state of being, which isn't acquired by a student; it is remembered. It is not something mysterious, but an intrinsic part of our natural potential. That we can use help in the process of remembering seems obvious and meaningful. A book alone is not sufficient, but it can be a means of support. I would recommend that anyone who really wants to go deeply into meditation take lessons at some stage. The enrichment of professional supervision and feedback cannot be substituted.

Everybody can learn to meditate. But meditation will not have the same meaning for everyone. It is like maths; everybody can learn to calculate (taking into account particular mental handicaps, which also apply to meditation), but not everyone will become a mathematician. Meditation is not suitable for everyone in terms of 'sitting down for it'. Some people spontaneously get into a meditative state; for example, during sports, or when they are creative in arts, or intimately together with a partner or a child, or in nature.

In this book, different methods of meditation are described, and examples are offered 'in action'. A brief description of the classical meaning of meditation, and different states of consciousness that can be experienced, is followed by suggestions for practice and an explanation of how to structure a meditation.

There are meditations with different themes and for different levels of experience. Each meditation is an infinite path; you may go further and further. In fact, I recommend that you practice the same meditation for a long period of time. A guideline could be: as long as you feel comfortable or as long as you feel you are getting something out of it. However, there is a pitfall! No development goes in a smooth straight line upwards; there will be peaks and dales and times that you make less progress; or – to your own perception – no progress at all. It will be tempting to try another method or technique, but perseverance and patience is needed here. Therefore, a second guideline could be: try every technique – if it appeals to you and this will not apply to every technique – for at least several weeks.

In many traditions, like, for example, in Zen and Transcendental Meditation, there is only one technique being taught, which is practised for years and years. Each method can lead to self-realisation. The versatility being offered in this book is meant to allow development of the versatility of the personality. It will also teach you to know the versatility of meditation, in order to take out of it what suits you best.

Usually, there are several meditations described, belonging to one theme, which are indicated by successive Roman Numerals. In some cases, these numbers indicate different approaches to a theme, but they usually indicate different stages of deepening and can be practised successively.

The first meditations described in this book consist of several methods to bring you to the point of relaxation and concentration. In the following meditations, it is implicitly assumed that you build up these stages according to your own preference. It is important that you pay sufficient attention to each stage, until you have the feeling that you have mastered it more or less.

The meditations are described very soberly, as they can be orally accompanied. The page following a meditation consists of explanation and suggestions. You may read a meditation first carefully, study the suggestions and let it sink in before you practice in silence. Or you may record your meditations. You can include periods of silence which, as long as you find comfortable and in the course of weeks, you may extend. In this way you can create your own programme.

It can be very stimulating to meditate with others, where one person may guide the meditation, or the exercise can be studied together beforehand and practiced together in silence.

I
Meditation

A Definition

To come to an original understanding of meditation, we consider the *Yoga-Sutras* (Taimni, 1961), a work which has been put in writing by Patanjali about two centuries B.C., but the wisdom goes back many centuries before that and has been taught by oral tradition. In these sutras, the classical philosophy of yoga is expounded and meditation is part of this. The following definition of yoga (and meditation) is given:

Yoga citta-vrtti-nirodha.
Yoga is the inhibition of the modifications of the mind.
(I, 2)

This is the literal Sanskrit translation according to Taimni. However, 'nirodha' (here being translated as 'inhibition') can also be translated as 'mastery', which implies mastering the skill to discipline the mind. 'Vrtti' can be translated as 'ways of existing', 'states', 'transformations', or 'movements'. So, one could as well say:

Yoga is the mastery of the movements within the mind.

This brings us to a workable definition: **yoga is the mastery of the mind**. All yoga is about the mastery of the mind! Physical exercises, breathing exercises are preludes, preparations to meditation, which is about the discipline of the mind.

The yoga of Patanjali consists of eight steps, of which the last four describe four different stages of meditation and the first four could be considered as a preparation to meditation. (II, 29) These eight steps are:

Yamas	Ethical principles of self-restraint
Niyamas	Ethical principles of observances
Asanas	Body postures
Pranayama	Mastery of *prana* or breath
Pratyahara	Withdrawal of attention
Dharana	Concentration
Dhyana	Meditation*
Samádhi	Contemplation*

Yamas

Yamas are ethical principles of self-restraint in giving up certain habits. However, there is no judgement in the positive or negative in the Yoga Sutra's (Patanjali speaks of, '...painful or not-painful' (I, 5)). It is just that these patterns do not serve you and will bring forth painful consequences.

The principles of self-restraint comprise: abstention from violence, untruthfulness, theft, lack of self-control and acquisitiveness. These apply to all levels of functioning, which means in action, but also in speech and thought. Yamas can be considered as guidelines to sharpen your personality. Each yama may serve as a subject for meditation.

Niyamas

Niyamas are the ethical principles of observance: purity, contentment, austerity, self-study, and self-surrender to God. These too are applicable in thought, word and action and are each worth further meditation. When the yamas and niyamas are practiced earnestly, this will lead to a completely new way of being.

Asanas

These are the physical exercises which made yoga famous in the West. They serve to maintain the body in good health and condition, and offer a suitable way of relaxation. According to

Patanjali, the asanas are a preparation to meditation. However, there are other schools, which do not know such a preparation to meditation and it lies outside of the scope of this book to go deeper into the asanas.

Pranayama

These are exercises for the breath and the subtle 'prana' (or flow of energy), with which one may acquire further mastery over vitality. In its most simple form, the regulation of the breath can be used to come to deep relaxation and a sample of these are described in the first exercise in this book, as a preparation to meditation. A deeper understanding of the topic of Pranayama, however, lies outside of the scope of this book.

Pratyahara

This is the withdrawal of the senses and the direction of the attention inwards: a necessary step to prepare for concentration. The senses and the mind are usually directed outwards and are being coloured by all impressions. A main part of our daily awareness is occupied by processing impressions from the outer world. In doing so, our thoughts wander from one thing to the other. In pratyahara, the attention is withdrawn from the senses in order to be directed inwards. A practical aid in this process is to begin to practice meditation in a secluded space with few sensory stimuli, no sounds from outside, no distractive objects, a pleasant temperature, etc. The eyes are kept closed. However, meditation is a way of being aware, and the ability to withdraw from the senses at will needs to be applied in a world full of impressions. Then it will be possible to be in meditation while there is a full openness to external impressions without being distracted.

Dharana

Dharana means concentration, the ability to hold the focus

within a framework of a chosen object. This is to say, to keep the attention on what you have chosen without allowing yourself to be distracted. When the mind is firmly drawn inwards, as described under pratyahara, there might still be distraction from within one's own mind, thoughts and emotions whirling around. In concentration, the attention is focussed and maintained.

Dhyana

Dhyana means meditation, and the explanation (according to Patanjali) is the ability to focus the attention single-pointedly. This means not only to stay with one object, but to hold just one image, one thought in one's awareness. The concentration is compiled to one point so that he/she is much more powerful. This is comparable to striking the point of a spike or a drawing pin; the force with which it is hit is much stronger in the point, because the surface is smaller, so that the spike is being forced into the wall. In a similar way, the mind can enter into a deeper level of awareness by the single-pointed force of meditation.

Samádhi

Samádhi is what is sometimes called higher meditation: becoming one with the object by going beyond the awareness of the 'I' and beyond mental limitations. There remains nothing in consciousness but the object and there is no awareness of the duality between the 'I' and the object. One becomes the subject, so to speak, and, in this way, one acquires direct knowledge.

The nearest definition of this kind of direct knowledge in our language is intuition. Intuition, for most of us, is something which may happen to us from time to time in a glimpse and which seems not always reliable. In our society, we don't learn how to use our intuition. We have not been trained in direct perception, and intuition is often clouded by emotions, desires and thoughts.

Patanjali speaks about three kinds of knowledge: the first

kind is called 'sabda' and means knowledge obtained by hearing through others; for example, the gossip of the neighbours, but also in the educational system, or by reading a book; it is taking the truth as others tell it. The second kind is called 'jnana': knowledge obtained by sensory information or by logical conclusion. This is the basis of science, experimental research and logical thinking of the abstract mind. The third and highest kind of knowledge is called 'artha', which literally means 'essence'. This is knowledge obtained by direct perception, or direct knowing. This is the knowledge obtained in samádhi.

This is what meditation is finally about: to develop direct knowing, the highest form of knowledge, the essence.

In the Yoga Sutras, Patanjali describes the way of meditation to be:

...established in your own essential and fundamental nature. (I, 3)

In this book, we refer to this 'own essential and fundamental nature' with the term 'the Self', also called 'the transpersonal Self'.

The term 'transpersonal' was first used by the psychologist Carl Jung and refers to an aspect in every human being, which stretches out beyond personal consciousness. The Self can be seen as a spiritual core of our being, our most pure individuality and, simultaneously, it is universal. In different cultures, different terminologies are used. The Self is often exchanged with the soul, which adds other connotations, which want to be avoided here.

In Sanskrit, the Self is translated as 'Atma': a concept stretching beyond the personality with emotions and thoughts. Atma has individual and universal aspects, which are basically one.

In other states there is assimilation of the Seer with the modifications of the mind. (I, 4)

The Seer is you, and the modifications of the mind are all changes in consciousness. This brings us to the original definition of meditation: 'Meditation is the mastery of the movements of the mind.' The art is to master our mind and not to identify with it, but to realise what our true nature is.

Samádhi is a state of awareness in which one's true nature can be known, but samádhi is not one stable state; it is a continuum of different states and dimensions, which I will describe briefly to give you an idea of what is possible with the mind and to give signposts that you may recognise in your own meditations.

Please realise that descriptions and definitions in words are limited and can fail these experiences, which stretch far beyond the realms of mental awareness.

This is a brief explanation of the phases described by Patanjali (I, 17). Apart from the last one, they belong to samprajnata samádhi, which means 'higher knowing'.

Mental Awareness

Assuming that one has brought their awareness to single-point-edness through concentration and meditation, one's awareness increases and moves into higher sub-planes of the mental plane, and reaches vitarka samádhi. This state is characterised by contemplation; the mind is still and clear and reflection on mental impressions is possible. You can take a question or problem into this state and an answer may be found by enhanced clarity and focus. There is no daily thinking, but direct and original insight. This state is called 'higher mental' and may sometimes occur spontaneously in sudden flashing insights.

Higher Mental or Causal Awareness

When awareness expands further, it enters the dimension of the causal plane (sometimes called the causal body) and vicara samádhi develops. This state is characterised by a sense of expansion and/or ascension. This is an illusion, which develops because one's awareness and thus one's energy field or aura expands. This state may occur spontaneously in, what is called in psychology, 'peak moments'.

This state of mind brings a feeling of immense joy, an increasing clarity and influx of inspiration.

Buddhic Awareness

At some point, the expanding movement alters in a receptive movement, and awareness moves into the buddhic dimension: the dimension of wisdom, intuition and compassion. This is called ananda samádhi and is characterised by a sense of bliss or delight. There is a realisation of connection and oneness with cosmic awareness and this gives a sense of bliss, as received from the cosmos, which, in fact, is the case. This state, too, may occur spontaneously in the form of so-called 'mystical experiences'.

This state of mind frees the individual from existential loneliness and enhances the capacity for love and the feeling of interconnectedness with the surrounding world.

Atmic Awareness

Then a balance will develop, along with a profound silence, a deafening silence. There is nothing but peace and a realisation of pure being: a sense of 'I am'. This is asmita samádhi, which literally means 'I am that'. It is the dimension earlier referred to as the dimension of Self. It is our most pure individual core and, simultaneously, it is transpersonal and universal. It is beyond ego or the concept of 'I', which has personal wishes for the individual and separated self. At the atmic plane, or Self, the self is inseparably connected with the universe and the One Mind and the concerns of the self are imbedded in the larger whole.

This state of mind is releasing the bonds of the ego, or lower self, and strengthening the awareness of one's essence: the Higher Self.

Awareness Without Seed

Beyond the Self, there is no content of awareness anymore; this is called nirbija samádh. It is characterised by the absence of realisation of 'I'. Awareness is empty, clear and infinite. There is no seed from which vrittis move, and transformations of the mind may sprout.

This state of mind is deeply purifying.

Beyond this there is dharma megha, in which awareness is absorbed in the cosmic and where origin and destination are one. One could say that beyond the infinite emptiness is infinite fullness, where everything originates.

This state of being is all-encompassing...

We naturally return from this state of 'awareness without seed' to our daily consciousness, because of the samskaras or seeds that our consciousness still carry and which produce thoughts, emotions and actions.

In the transitions between one state and another there is asamprajnata samádhi. In this, there is no content of awareness, like in the ones described above. Awareness is drawn inside, focussed on nothing but itself, which causes it to transcend to a more subtle dimension and finally into awareness without seed.

This is the rough 'map' of the dimensions of our awareness in samádhi. In this book, no more can be said about it; these are experiences, which need to be felt and taught by teacher to student. However, it is possible to reach samádhi via all meditations described in this book. When you recognise some of the descriptions above, it may be time to find professional guidance to further development.

Samyama

Finally, concentration, meditation and samádhi may happen

simultaneously and become integrated. This state of being is called samyama. In samyama it is possible to be doing something concentrated, with single-pointed attention and expanding consciousness beyond duality, with direct knowing. This can be during action here and now.

Meditation is not only a way to expand one's own awareness; it is also a way to be fully present in life. It is not only a way inward; it is a way outward. This is described in the sequence of exercises 'Mindfulness'.

NB. Be aware that these descriptions of concentration, meditation and contemplation are indications of different qualities of consciousness. This tells nothing about the method which is used. There are numerous methods and techniques for meditation and in this book you will find a small selection. In the end, meditation is a quality of being which can be lived.

*In the English version of I.K.Taimni, dhyana is translated as 'contemplation' and samádhi as 'trance'. I find this disturbing and in contradiction with the original meaning of the Sanskrit word. Because of this, I have chosen to translate dhyana as 'meditation' and to use the original term Samádhi as much as possible.

Practice

Intention

Why do you want to meditate? What do you want to accomplish with your meditation? What is your motivation, your intention? Meditation has a different meaning for everyone. One may want to relax and find inner peace and silence. Another may want to explore personal growth, expand one's awareness and learn to use it creatively, or to resolve certain problems, to get rid of fears, or gaining insights. Sometimes, someone wants to meditate to contribute something to others. It's all possible.

Intention is a basic attitude, and, as such, it is comparable with the moral principles of Patanjali.

Next, there is the question: What are you willing to give? What is your effort to make this intention come true?

As described in Patanjali:

Samádhi is nearest to those whose desire for Samádhi is intensely strong. (I, 21)

And also:

A further differentiation arises by reason of the mild, medium and intense nature of means employed. (I, 22)

In other words, reward is given according to effort. However, there is another factor involved:

Or by self-surrender to God. (I, 23).

Surrender

The degree of surrender, which correlates directly with the intention with which you meditate, is also determining the experience. This is even more important than the effort you make in terms of time investment. Are you really going for it? Or are you holding back? Often enough, a part of us wants to, but right under the surface there are all kinds of resistances, which prevent you from going for it: tiredness, business, laziness, restlessness and so many other things to do. Investigate these resistances; they keep you from reaching your goal.

Discipline

Meditation requires discipline, without an association of heaviness of hard work and struggle. It is like a game, with a delicate balance between effort and surrender, giving and receiving. It is like walking a tightrope, balancing between fields of force. Therefore, practice is different for everyone. A natural discipline will develop when the wish to meditate has come from within and is not a self-imposed thought, 'because it seems to be good for me'. Discipline is not 'I have to'; discipline is focussed effort, because there is a wish, because it is fun. Discipline only works when meditation is fun. And it is, or rather it can be. It can be made as pleasant or challenging as you choose it to be.

To get an idea of what meditation is – to let meditation be truly meditation – some training is necessary. Everyone can meditate; one may have more natural skill than another, but everyone can learn it; yet, it does require practice. And in order to practice, here are some suggestions:

Place

Choose a place where you feel comfortable and where you will not be disturbed. Preferably, use the same place each time, which will not be used for other purposes, so that you will associate this place with meditation. This can also be the same mat or blanket where you sit, even though this mat will be put in different spots.

Time

If possible, meditate each day at the same time. By doing so, you will create a rhythm, by which meditation will more easily become a natural part of your life. A classical ideal is the moment of sunrise or sunset, but this is not always practical. Good alternatives are the moments in the morning before you start the day and in the evening at the end of your (working) day (both or one of those). Take into account your bio-rhythm; some people's minds are most clear in the mornings, others in the evenings.

Duration of Time

In the beginning, it is recommendable to meditate more often and for a shorter period of time, instead of now and then for a long time. This is to maintain and to train concentration. Ten minutes twice a day is fine to start with; gradually, this can be extended twenty minutes, half an hour, or even an hour, whatever you feel comfortable with.

Ritual

For some people, it works fine to let the meditation be preceded by a ritual, in order to build up concentration. This may be, for example, lighting a candle, listening to a piece of music, or doing some relaxation or breathing exercises. This is entirely according to one's own preference.

Position

The body posture during meditation is performed according to personal preference and possibilities. Patanjali says of this that:

Posture should be steady and comfortable. (II, 46)

This means that the body should not cause any hindrance during meditation, but should be relaxed, quiet and steady. The classical position is to sit up straight, with crossed legs, on the floor or on a firm cushion. Once you are trained in this posture, it perfectly meets the description of being steady, balanced and comfortable. But when your body is not so trained, you may as well suffice with a straight position on a chair. To keep the back straight is advisable in order to stay alert and not to develop any tension in the back or shoulders. To lie down straight on bed or on the floor is an alternative. This has a disadvantage that you may fall asleep more easily, but this too differs from person to person and there are people who are well able meditate while lying down.

It can be pleasant to move a bit in advance, through sport, or relaxation exercises, so that your body will be able to rest. Keep in mind that the asanas in the eight steps of Patanjali are a preparation to meditation.

Risks

Meditation is basically a natural state of consciousness, which is expanding and healing. Nevertheless, there is a chance of some risks while practicing, which one needs to be aware of, especially when one meditates without a teacher. When you meditate too much and for too long a period of time (read: fanaticism) you can strain yourself too much, with the following possible consequences: headache, dizziness and psychic instability. To people who are somewhat instable, mentally or emotionally, this is a higher risk. If you fall into this category and you want to meditate – and meditation can very well be used therapeutically – it is best done under professional supervision.

When is it too much and too long? When you are forcing yourself, and why should you? Have a closer look at your motives and intention.

Our consciousness has an enormous potential and needs to be dealt with cautiously.

How to Structure a Meditation

The structure of a meditation may differ according to the method. In the meditations described in this book, there is a general line maintained based on the steps of Patanjali:

Relaxation and Concentration

In each description of a meditation in this book, it is implicitly assumed that you have taken a comfortable body posture and the description starts with closing the eyes. Then there is the first stage of deepening the relaxation, sometimes followed by attention for the breath, next the withdrawal of the attention inwards and building the concentration. This stage may suffice as an independent exercise for the beginning practitioner.

Meditation

Next, there is the second stage, in which deepening of concentration into meditation takes place and consciousness is being directed single-pointedly. Mental force is being bundled to a strong potential, which may lead to the experience of deep silence and insight, and may be used for affirmation, visualisation and creative ability.

Samádhi

In the third stage, one can transcend the mental level into the realm of insight, intuition and direct knowing, in which one comes in conscious contact with the Self. This is called higher meditation or samádhi. There are several sub-stages to be distinguished; the lower of which are suitable to obtain insight into questions or problems, by taking them beyond rational thinking. In this way, it is possible to come to a fuller understanding of one's purpose. One may also connect with the source of unconditional love of the higher Self and full acceptance of oneself and others. Above all, this is the stage where one may transcend one's personal reality. This is transpersonal and goes beyond imagination, beyond images and forms, beyond words and thoughts, beyond time and space. One may connect to Universal Love, the Absolute and complete silence.

To Return to Daily Awareness

One returns to daily awareness with the intention to end the meditation. Let go of the experience; focus the attention on the physical body again; feel the weight of the body; feel the connection with the ground; feel the hands and the feet; take a few deep breaths; stretch out and open the eyes.

II

Meditations

Concentration and Meditation

This first sequence of meditations is the classical form of concentration and meditation, according to the definition of Patanjali. This is the path of growing awareness. The more experienced you are, the more the exercises will lead you into, what is called, higher meditation or samádhi.

The sequence consists of different stages of deepening, indicated by a Roman Numeral. The sequence, 'Breath', 'Space' and 'Silence', are beginning exercises for concentration, which may also serve as a preparation for later meditations.

In 'A Seed-thought' and 'An Object', techniques are presented to deepen the concentration. In 'Concentration', a specific technique is presented of structure and alignment. In 'The Self', contact is made with an essential aspect of us: the transpersonal Self. And finally, in the sequence 'Mindfulness', meditation is to be applied in daily life.

I

Breath I

Close your eyes
and focus attention inwards.
Observe your breathing
in and out, in and out.
Feel the breath
deep under in your belly.
Lay the hands on the lower belly
and feel how the belly expands
at an inhalation
and pulls inwards
at an exhalation
in and out, in and out.
Follow the movement of the breath
with the hands
and with attention.
Let all tension flow out
at an exhalation.
Allow relaxation to come
at an inhalation.
Allow the physical body
to come to rest
in this movement.
When it is sufficient
let go of the focus.
Feel the weight of your body.
Breathe in and out three times more.
Stretch out
and open your eyes.

Suggestions

This is a good relaxation exercise for the physical body preceding a meditation, or as independent exercise for beginning practitioners. This exercise may be practiced for a week or longer, before you continue with 'Breath II'.

Stay alert and keep your attention to the breath. Do not breathe excessively. Do not force yourself in anything. Relaxation comes especially by focussing on the exhalation. The deeper the relaxation, the longer the exhalation naturally will be.

When you notice that your attention is wandering off, just go back to the breath. It might be that you are restless, which is common in the beginning when one tries to relax and be quiet, or it might be that you are trying to carry on with the exercise for too long. In this last case, you had better end the exercise.

2

Breath II

Close your eyes
and focus attention inwards.
Observe your breathing
in and out, in and out.
Feel the breath
deep under in your belly.
Allow the body to relax
in your exhalation.
Breathe on quietly.
Let the body be
and focus on your emotions.
Allow all emotions you are carrying with you
from the past day, week, period
to come up
while you breathe on quietly.
Experience the emotions;
observe them; accept them
and breathe them out.
Let them go at an exhalation
and allow rest and harmony to come
at an inhalation
in and out, in and out.
When it is sufficient
let go of the focus.
Feel the weight of your body.
Breathe in and out three times more.
Stretch out
and open your eyes.

Suggestions

Elaborating on the previous exercise, this one goes further with relaxation of the emotional plane. This plane can be seen as an energy field surrounding and penetrating the physical body. In yoga and in esoteric philosophy, it is called the emotional body. This image may be helpful in breathing in the emotional body and thus breathing emotions out.

NB. Emotions are not to be confused with feelings. Emotions are the feelings of the personality, while feeling is a sensing quality and, more expanded, it can also be related to the Self. Love, for example, is not an emotion; it is a quality of the Self, but love can generate emotions and can be communicated through emotions.

3

Breath III

Close your eyes
and focus attention inwards.
Observe your breathing
in and out, in and out.
Feel the breath
deep under in your belly.
Allow the body to relax
at an exhalation.
Allow all emotions you are carrying with you
to come up.
Experience them; observe them; accept them
and let them go at an exhalation.
Breathe on quietly.
When emotions have come to rest
let the emotions be
and focus on your thoughts.
Observe thoughts, images, impressions
coming up within you.
Observe them, accept them
and let them go at an exhalation.
Breathe them out
and allow silence and clarity to come
at an inhalation
in and out, in and out.
Breath with your whole being
in the stream of life.
Let go of what you do not longer need
in and out, in and out.

When it is sufficient
let go of the focus.
Feel the weight of your body.
When it is sufficient
let go of the focus.
Feel the weight of your body.
Breathe in and out three times more.
Stretch out
and open your eyes.

Suggestions

A step further than relaxation of the emotional body is relaxation of the mental body. The mental plane can also be seen as an energy field, stretching out beyond the emotional. By holding the focus on the breath, one can let go of thoughts. Together, these three exercises of 'Breath' form a good preparation for all meditations.

4

Space I

Close your eyes
and focus attention inwards.
Observe your breathing
in and out, in and out.
Experience the space
flowing in
at an inhalation
and flowing out
at an exhalation.
Feel the space
developing in the body.
Feel the space
you are creating in your body.
Feel the space
you are taking.
Take your space!
When it is sufficient
let go of the focus.
Feel the weight of your body.
Breathe in and out three times more.
Stretch out
and open your eyes.

Suggestions

This is a relaxation exercise to play with the concept of space.

I once heard meditation being defined as 'taking your own space'. In other words, being who you truly are. Some of us are afraid to take our own space, while others take more space than is theirs. This exercise helps you to be aware of your own space, to allow yourself to take it and to allow yourself to be.

5

Space II

Close your eyes
and focus attention inwards.
Observe your breathing
in and out, in and out.
Experience the space
flowing in
at an inhalation
and flowing out
at an exhalation.
Extend your attention
beyond the physical body.
Experience the space around.
Enclose this space
with your attention.
This is also your space.
You are taking this space
with your breath
with your emotions
with your thoughts.
Breathe in this space.
Let emotions
which are filling the space
come to rest.
Let all thoughts, images, impressions
which are filling the space
come to silence.
Let space be space

Suggestions

As an extension of the previous exercise, one's own space is now consciously being extended with the breath, emotions and thoughts. The principle of an emotional and mental body, as described in the 'Breath' exercises, is applicable here as well: the emotional and the mental bodies take space. We can become aware of this space. When we are full with emotions and thoughts, we do not experience inner space. This space can be created consciously.

6

Space III

Close your eyes
and focus attention inwards.
Observe your breathing
in and out, in and out.
Experience the space
flowing in
at an inhalation
flowing out
at an exhalation.
Experience the space in your body.
Extend your attention
beyond the physical body.
Experience the space around.
Enclose this space
with your attention.
Let all emotions, thoughts, and images,
which are filling the space
come to silence.
Let space be space.
Extend your attention
beyond your own space.
Stretch out beyond your 'I'
into the unknown.
Explore this space
with your consciousness.
Be present in this space.
Be aware of space.
Infinite space.

Suggestions

This meditation has a basic assumption that, when one stretches out beyond the borders of the personal, one enters a transpersonal dimension, which is infinite – a universal space with unlimited possibilities. This space can be experienced not with the mind, but with one's awareness; it is a sense, a way of feeling.

How does one transcend the borders of the 'I'?

It seems like a jump into the unknown, which we shall meet in other meditations too. Words are only signposts. Letting go is a keynote – trust and surrender...

Do you dare to cross the known borders of your own space and stretch your awareness beyond?

7

Silence I

Close your eyes
and focus attention inwards.
Observe your breathing
in and out, in and out.
Feel the flow of the breath
going through your body in waves.
Allow your body to rock on the waves
in and out, in and out.
Feel the emptiness
after and exhale.
Feel the fullness
after an inhalation
in and out.
Feel the moments of silence
in the emptiness and the fullness.
Listen to these moments of silence.
Allow the silence in.

Suggestions

This is a beginning meditation to become silent: silence within the movement of the breath. When you listen to the moments between an inhalation and an exhalation, these moments will be prolonged and the breath will become more quiet and deep. Let this happen without forcing it. Remain an observer; listen and feel.

8

Silence II

Close your eyes
and focus attention inwards.
Observe your breathing
in and out, in and out.
Let go of the breath
and allow the silence in.
Open yourself for everything
that may come up.
Do you start to feel uneasy?
Observe it.
Accept it
and let it be.
Are there any emotions coming up?
Observe them.
Accept them
and let them be.
Are there any thoughts coming up?
Observe them.
Accept them
and let them be.
Are there any images coming up?
Observe them.
Accept them
and let them be.
Is there silence?
Observe the silence.
Accept the silence
and let the silence be.

Listen to the silence.
Enter the silence.
Allow silence to enter into you.
Be present in silence.
Be still.

Suggestions

As soon as one becomes silent, one's consciousness will register all kinds of disturbances:

Impressions from outside: sounds, warmth, coldness.
Impressions from the body: discomfort, restlessness, stiffness, tingling sensations, itching.
Impressions from within: images, thoughts and emotions.

This happens with a beginning meditation. The mind is like a wild horse. To tame it while keeping its spirit one needs gentleness, acceptance, patience and discipline. To suppress the mind with the will, will have a contrary effect. The art is to let the disturbances be. Do not go along with them; be aware that you are the one who thinks, feels, sees. You are not your thoughts; you may have them, but you are not them. Observe objectively, like a spectator in an empty cinema who is watching a white screen, where all kinds of images are passing by.

When it becomes more silent, do not think or report to yourself: 'Hey, it is silent!' That is another thought and it is not silent anymore. Let it be and be part of it.

9

Silence III

Close your eyes
and focus attention inwards.
Observe your breathing
in and out, in and out.
Allow the breath to flow out.
Allow the silence in.
Open yourself for everything
that may come up.
Let emotions, thoughts and images be
what they are.
Let them go.
Allow silence to be.
Be in silence.
Be still.
In silence
you'll find reality
beyond name and form,
beyond emptiness and fullness –
reality as it is –
the source
of insight and wisdom.
Be still and know.

Suggestions

This cryptic description is another signpost. When it is and remains completely silent, you are beyond the mental plane; beyond the 'I'; beyond imagination; beyond words. Only when there is silence will you be able to listen to the knowing which lies beyond. In many philosophies and religions, one speaks of 'reality as it is'. This is an experience not to be communicated through words.

10

An Object

In Nature
Sit down in front of a flower (plant, tree, animal, stone, etc).
Allow the body, emotions and thoughts to relax
and become silent.
Watch the flower.
Take in all its details.
Open yourself.
Look beyond the outer appearance of the flower.
Look into the essence of the being of the flower.
Connect with the essence.
Become one with the flower.
Become the flower.
Experience the flower from within.
Be a flower.

Suggestions

For this meditation it would be good if you were prepared by the sequence of 'Space' and 'Silence' meditations. One needs have inner space and a still mind in order to be able to truly listen to nature and to merge with it. If possible, do this meditation outside, in and with nature itself. Beside one single tangible object you can also focus on a forest, a species of plants - or animals, a mountain, a river, the sea, or the wind. Do not be afraid of imagination. Accept that imagination may be part of it. And realise that energy follows thought. Try not to have any expectations and do not interpret your experiences.

11

A Seed-thought I

Close your eyes.
Breathe in and out quietly and deeply.
Relax your physical body
and take in your awareness a seed-thought.
See the image before you.
Hear the word.
Repeat it in your thoughts
and – if you like – aloud.
Keep your consciousness focussed
and keep on repeating it.
Direct your attention to the meaning
of your seed-thought
and to the meaning behind the meaning.
Get through to the essence
beyond the image
beyond the word
beyond the meaning.
Experience your seed-thought into the dimension of the Self.
Let your seed-thought carry you
to the source.

Suggestions

A seed-thought is meant to be a basic idea, a rudiment or archetype. It may also be a symbol or visual image.

When you choose a seed-thought for your meditation, the meaning that it has for you is important. It is the intention with which you meditate. Choose a word, image or saying that touches you and on which you can sharpen your mind.

The Yamas and Niyamas are suitable for this meditation; for example: harmlessness, truth, self-discipline, non-acquisitiveness, purity, contentment, austerity, self-study and self-surrender (to God).

There are other principles suitable as seed-thoughts; for instance:

Light	Awareness	Strength
Peace	Openness	Courage
Joy	Honesty	Responsibility
Freedom	Clarity	Flexibility
Love	Faith	Humour
Compassion	Forgiveness	Creativity
Gratitude	Communication	Playfulness
Synthesis	Purpose	Abundance
Beauty	Truth	

One advantage of using a seed-thought is that it helps to focus the consciousness single-pointedly, so that disturbances coming from outside, as well as within, naturally cease to exist. All concentration is directed to the seed-thought and a deep relaxation will evolve. As the activity of the mind is purely mental, you may reflect on the meaning of the seed-thought. You may get all kinds of associations around it. Gradually, however, your consciousness will become single-pointed in meditation. There will be nothing, but the seed-thought in image, word or meaning. You will penetrate the outer appearance and get an understanding of the deeper personal meaning that this particular seed-thought has for you. This is an understanding in the dimension of the Self. When this happens, your awareness may stretch further out, beyond the word, beyond the image, beyond the meaning, and it will become one with the essence, the universal value of the seed-thought. This is samádhi.

Meditation on a seed-thought is related to meditation on a mantra. The original meaning of a 'mantra' is a holy saying or word to repeat. Holy can be understood as a word with a deeper meaning. By meditating on it, one may expand one's awareness and touch upon the divine.

In India, a mantra is traditionally passed on by the teacher to the student; usually, it is a word or saying out of the holy Sanskrit texts. This is personally chosen for the student and is meant to help him/her on his/her path. It is not a magic word; although the classical mantras carry a certain vibration, by being repeated throughout the ages with such a devotion and dedication. This applies to certain prayers as well.

Transcendental Meditation uses mantras. And in Zen-tradition, one knows the use of a koan, a paradoxical riddle, given by the teacher to the student to transcend ordinary thinking and to come to a unique answer by an expanded awareness.

The three following meditations are examples of meditations on a seed-thought.

12

A Seed-thought II

Peace
Close your eyes
Breathe in and out quietly and deeply.
Take 'peace' as a seed-thought in your awareness.
Reflect on the meaning of peace at a physical level
for you personally and for the world.
And allow your physical body to relax in peace.
Reflect on the meaning of peace at emotional level
(peace in emotions)
for you personally and for the world.
Allow your emotions come to peace.
Reflect on the meaning of peace at a mental level
(peace in thoughts)
for you personally and for the world.
Allow your thoughts to become peaceful.
Go beyond the word 'peace'.
Direct your attention towards the Self.
Experience the peace of the level of the Self,
your transpersonal Self, the universal Self.
Experience the deeper value of peace.
Be in peace.
Be peace.

Suggestions

This is a very classical meditation, to which there are numerous possible variations. Peace is complementary to the first *yama*, 'abstention from violence', or harmlessness. It is a positive rephrasing of the same principle.

Peace is a quality of the Self. On the level of the Self, violence does not exist, for there is no experience of duality and separation and there is no dissonance. What is done to another is – from the perspective of Self – done to ourselves. When we are capable of integrating the experience of oneness and of peace into our personality, we will not be able to commit violence anymore, either in action, in words or in thoughts.

13

A Seed-thought III

Beauty
Close your eyes
Breathe in and out quietly and deeply.
Relax your body.
Take 'beauty' as a seed-thought in your awareness.
Reflect on the meaning of beauty at a physical level
(physical beauty)
(beauty of emotions)
(beauty of thoughts)
in your life and your being.
Allow yourself to be beautiful
as you are.
Go beyond the word 'beauty'.
Direct your attention to the Self.
Experience the beauty of the Self.
Allow the Self to be, in all your beauty.
See beauty in imperfection.
See beauty without judgement.
See beauty in all life.

Suggestions

Beauty is also a quality of the Self. Beauty is an inner quality, which may manifest in the outer world. It is an art to be able to see beauty in the world. And it is an art to be able to make beauty visible, to let hidden beauty come out. This is the task to which an artist sets him/herself; in our core we are all artists. In some outer appearances, beauty is more obvious than in others. But when you look behind the outer appearance, you may see beauty in its true nature. This meditation is dedicated to the beauty in us all.

14

A Seed-thought IV

Truth
Close your eyes.
Breathe in and out quietly and deeply.
Relax your body.
Take 'truth' as a seed-thought in your awareness.
Reflect on the meaning of truth.
What does 'truth' mean to you?
What is true?
Go beyond the word 'truth'.
Direct your attention to the Self.
Experience the truth of the Self.
Listen to the Self to learn your own truth.
Only by following your truth
will you come to universal truth.
Align your thoughts, words and actions
to your highest truth.

Suggestions

Truth is also a quality of the Self. It requires discernment to be able to see what is true; what is true for one person is not necessarily true for another. Truth is related to a reality frame, to a certain dimension. As human beings, we each live in our own reality frames. And we exist with our consciousness in different dimensions. Once we become aware of this, we are able to make a choice for the truth we want to follow, the truth we chose to live. Expanding your awareness of truth is expanding your reality frame and becoming aware of a higher truth, another higher truth, and another...

15

Concentration I

Close your eyes
Focus on your breath
and allow your body to relax
at every exhalation.
Allow emotions to come to rest
at every exhalation.
Allow thoughts to become silent
at every exhalation.
Observe your breath
in the area of the heart.
Be aware of the heart as a centre*
of energy of unconditional love
and, as such, an intrinsic part of your being.
Sense the quality.
Sense the vibration.
Allow it to expand.
Hold your focus in your heart-centre.
Sense and observe.
Be in your heart.

Suggestions

This meditation starts a sequence, which has the aim to build concentration and to align and to centre the different dimensions of our being. It is a sequence of exercise for more experienced practitioners and it is not entirely without risks, because the attention is directed within one's own system. When this is done on willpower, one may create damage to oneself. Do the exercise with loving attention. The purpose is to be aware of this centre, not to manipulate anything.

*It is being suggested here that you observe the breath in the area of the heart and to sense the heart as a centre, also known as chakra. The heart-centre is an energy centre in the heart area, related to the heart organ. From an esoteric point of view, the heart-centre is a centre of love and wisdom. One could say that the heart chakra is the psychic heart. It has the capacity for compassion, unconditional love, inner wisdom, intuition, higher intelligence, interconnectedness and responsibility. By withdrawing the attention into the heart-centre, one centres oneself. It is in this centre that you can withdraw without excluding yourself from the world, meeting the world from a secure base of strength and love. The heart-centre is directly connected to the higher Self.

One finds the meaning of the heart-centre in proverbs and expressions, like 'With heart and soul', 'With all my heart', 'From the deepest of my heart', 'Speaking from the heart', 'Knowing in the heart', 'Connected from heart to heart', 'To know someone's heart.'

16

Concentration II

Close your eyes.
Focus your attention on your breath
and allow your body, emotions and thoughts to relax
and become silent
at every exhalation.
Observe the breath
in the area of the heart
and sense the heart as a centre.
Connect the heart with the ajna centre*
and move your attention
towards your forehead.
Sense your forehead as a centre
of pure mental energy.
Find the point in the middle of ajna*
And withdraw your attention here.
Focus on this point
of concentrated mental force.
Allow it to expand
and hold it
in silence.

Suggestions

You are being asked here to make a connection between the heart and the head: feeling and intellect. You may take your time to experience this connection before you move on.

*Ajna centre is the point in the middle of your forehead. This is the energetic centre related to the higher aspect of the mental plane: the plane of abstract thinking. This point is situated in the area of the pituitary gland and can be found by drawing an imaginative line from the root of the nose (in-between the eyebrows) backwards and from the tips of your ears inwards. The cross point of these lines is the middle point of the forehead centre. Once you have found it, it feels like a 'click', like two magnets clicking together. When the attention can be steadily held in this point, this will give a sensation of space in the head and often a perception of light. Sometimes, some pressure may be developed, as if the head is getting bigger. This is the ajna centre, which is expanding when one focuses one's attention there.

By withdrawing one's consciousness into ajna, concentration and mental clarity are enhanced, which is the purpose of this exercise. It is a good independent exercise to build up concentration and mental strength. Alternatively, this exercise can be used as a preparation for further meditation.

N.B. When focussing attention in the ajna, do so with love, attention and not with the will! The purpose is to become aware of this centre and not to manipulate anything.

17

Concentration III

Close your eyes.
Focus your attention on your breath
and allow your body, emotions and thoughts to relax
and become silent
at every exhalation.
Observe the breath
in the area of the heart
and sense the heart as a centre.
Connect the heart with the ajna centre
and move your attention
towards the middle point of ajna.
Hold your attention in this point
in silence.
Connect ajna and crown*
and heart and crown.
Direct your attention
to a point straight above the crown.
Feel the crown as a centre.
Sense the quality.
Allow it to expand.
Hold your focus in this point
in silence.

Suggestions

* The crown centre or crown chakra is the centre straight above the physical crown. The middle point of this centre is situated slightly above the physical crown of the skull. This centre is the gateway to the dimension of the soul. Here, one is able to connect to the buddhic realm of intuition, the Atmic realm of Self and even the higher realms (see page 19). When consciousness is withdrawn in this centre, intuition and awareness of one's inner source is being enhanced. The silence in this awareness can be deepened and another way of perception will develop, which is more expansive and inclusive. Spontaneous insights may come up.

It is recommendable to connect the heart centre to the ajna centre, to the crown centre as described in order to

N.B. When attention is focussed in the crown centre, do this with love, loving attention and not with the will! The purpose is to become aware of this centre and not to manipulate anything.

18

Concentration IV

Close your eyes.
Focus your attention on your breath
and allow your body, emotions and thoughts to relax
and become silent.
At every exhalation
Withdraw in your heart-centre.
Connect heart and ajna.
Focus in the middle point of ajna
and hold your attention in this point
in silence.
Connect ajna and crown centre
and heart and crown centre.
Direct your attention
to your crown centre.
Hold your focus in this point
in silence.
Stretch your attention further out
in a straight line upwards
and downwards.
Think and sense the line.
Connect crown and base centre.*
Stretch out further
straight up into the sky
and down into the earth.
Hold your concentration
on this line.
Sense this line.
It's a line of light,**

a central axis of your being,
a spiritual spine,
a source of strength.

Suggestions

The base centre, or base chakra, is an energetic centre situated at the bottom end of your spine. It is related to basic needs of survival and basic emotional needs, like safety. It is the centre where one can ground oneself and connect to the earth.

**This is called a 'line of light' and it is perceivable as such. When you withdraw your consciousness in this line, from crown to base centre and stretching out from here straight up and downwards, you will strengthen your spiritual will or intention. It is the intention of the higher Self to manifest itself in life; it is the will to live, the central axis of our human being and it manifests the spiritual Will-to-Be. Once you can anchor your consciousness here, you may experience purpose. In other words: your personal purpose in life. This will bring you in contact with your own source and your original strength.

This meditation can be practised either seated or standing. When you stand, stand with the legs slightly apart, feet in line with your hips, back straight, without overstretching it. The line can be experienced clearly this way and there will be a profound grounding.

19

Concentration V

Close your eyes.
Focus your attention on your breath
and allow your body, emotions and thoughts to relax
and become silent
at every exhalation.
Withdraw in your heart-centre.
Connect heart and ajna.
Focus in the middle point of ajna.
Connect ajna and crown centre
and heart and crown centre.
Hold your focus in your crown centre
in silence.
Stretch your attention out
in a straight line upwards
and downwards.
Connect crown and base
and stretch out further
straight up into the sky
and down into the earth.
Hold your concentration
in the line of your centre
and move your focus
upwards along the line.
Do this with the intention
of expanding your awareness.
Surrender
to the unknown.

Suggestions

This line of your core is like a spiritual anchor; it helps you to stay grounded and it may serve you to further expand your awareness. It may also serve as a preparation to the meditation 'The Self'. There are infinite dimensions to explore and I choose not to describe them here, as your own experience is more valuable. So, words are once again meant to be just signposts to lead you to your own experience. The purity of the intention with which one enters into meditation determines the quality of the experience. Surrender is necessary. One should not want to stay in control. There is nothing to be afraid of; you are entirely safe. Nothing will happen outside of the will of the Self.

20

The Self I

Close your eyes
and focus your attention within.
Ask yourself the question:
'Who am I?'
Let the question reverberate
into the very core of your being,
a memory of the Self,
and move towards this.
Experience who you are
and ask yourself:
'Is this really who I am?'
Let go of that
which does not feel true.
You don't need it.
'This is not who I am;
that is not who I am.'
Let go of
emotions, thoughts, images.
They are not
who you truly are.
You may have them
but you are them not.
Move on
your intention
directed towards your true Self

Suggestions

In this meditation, the intention to get to know your Self is the point of departure. The underlying assumption is that there is a way of knowing the Self and each step on this way is valuable in itself. When we want to get to know our Self, we do not necessarily meet our higher Self immediately. Allow yourself time. Be prepared to encounter the darkest parts of your ego: your small 'I' first. Allow and accept that!

Acknowledge your small ego; it has its function in building an instrument for survival in this world. Your ego creates an identity, but realise that this is not who you truly are! In course of your path, your ego is inhibiting you from moving forward by its fears and attachments. Your ego is a created construct and not who you truly are: not your Self.

The principle, 'This is not who I am; that is not who I am', is called the principle of 'neti-neti'. This literally means, 'Not this, not that'. It is to acquire the ability of discernment, to distinguish between the real and the unreal by letting go of what is unreal.

Suppose one has pain, either a toothache or sorrow about a loved one. There is the realisation that I am not my pain. I have pain, but I am not pain. The pain is acknowledged, accepted, but there is no identification with the pain. The deeper one's awareness of the Self, the greater the ability to put things into perspective and the more the detachment from the worries and hassles of the ego personality. This is simply because there are more essential experiences known.

*More explanation about the Self is in chapter 1: Meditation: a definition, under Samádhi.

21

The Self II

Close your eyes
and focus your attention within.
Experience who you are.
Let go of that
which does not feel true.
'This is not who I am;
that is not who I am.'
Let go of
emotions, thoughts, images.
They are not
who you truly are.
You may have them
but you are not them.
It becomes silent,
a deafening silence,
a deep peace,
an unconditional love,
and you know:
'This is who I am.
I have come home.
I am.'

Suggestions

When all 'unrealities' have been released, nothing remains but absolute silence. It is an easy exercise to describe, but not easy to carry out. The state of consciousness which develops is described by Patanjali as 'asmita-samádhi' and is distinguished by a silence, so intense that it is called deafening: a deep peace and an all-embracing unconditional love, disrobed of any emotion or attachment (see page 19). Often, there is a perception of light or whiteness, like the feeling of a silent grand plain of virgin snow. When this state of consciousness manifests, there is an awareness of 'I am', without any personal charge; it is pure awareness of individuality. This state of consciousness is very healing, trans-forming and stabilising. Once one has experienced this, one knows what self-awareness is; one is aware of one's true worth. One knows the transpersonal Self, unique and at the same time not more or less than any other Self, which leads to self-esteem, as well as unconditional respect for others.

A lack of self-esteem, self-love and self-confidence lies at the bottom of so many illnesses of the personality, thus resulting in aggression, denunciation, discrimination and suppression of oneself as well as others, in order to make a small 'I' seem bigger. Meeting the Self opens to another perspective of oneself and of the world.

22

The Self III

Beyond the Self
Close your eyes
and focus your attention within.
Experience who you are.
Let go of that
which does not feel true.
'This is not who I am;
that is not who I am.'
Until it becomes silent,
a deafening silence,
a deep peace,
an unconditional love,
and you know:
'This is who I am.
I have come home
I am.'
There is an intention
to go to the source
beyond 'I am'.
Let go of 'I am'.
let go of yourself.
Go beyond
the borders of self.
Surrender
to the unknown.
Emptiness.
A leap into the dark.
Emptiness is fullness.

There is nothing but Self.
Self becomes Transpersonal Self
becomes Universal Self
'I am' becomes
'Being'.

Suggestions

The intention to return to the source is an existential longing. One could say a divine homesickness. It is a rudimentary memory of where we come from and of who we truly are.

To become aware of this, one needs to let go of all that is known, also the 'I am'. This experience goes beyond individual consciousness; it is universal, unlimited and all-encompassing.

Beyond the I is the universal.

'Be still and know: I am God.'

23

Mindfulness I

Keep your eyes open
and look at what you are seeing.
Be aware of your ears
and listen to what you are hearing.
Be aware of your skin
and feel what you are touching.
Be aware of your tongue
and taste what you are tasting.
Be aware of your nose
and smell what you are smelling.
Now be aware of all your senses
as gates between you and the world.
See, hear, sense, taste and smell.
Be aware of yourself
being part of the world.
Be mindful.
Be still in all.

Suggestions

Mindfulness means being aware of what you are doing. This is another line of meditation, complementary to the line of concentration. Mindfulness meditation is not a concentration on one object, but attention to everything, or, if you like, concentration on everything. Contrary to all previous meditations, this is a meditation where you do not withdraw inside yourself, but remain consciously part of the environment. It is an exercise to remain aware in the here and now, to have a still mind, but a mind which is fully alert. This is possible with one's awareness in concentration meditation, as well as in samádhi.

Finally, mindfulness meditation, as well as concentration meditation, will lead to oneness and universal awareness.

24

Mindfulness II

Be mindful in the world.
Allow all impressions to be
and encompass them all.
Allow images from within,
emotions, thoughts.
Let them be.
Be aware
yet do not give them any thought.
Be mindful
but let your mind be empty.
Embrace them with your awareness
without identifying with them.
You are not your senses.
You are not your body.
You are not your emotions.
You are not your thoughts.
They serve you
to be in the world.
Be silent
and be a part of reality
as it is.
Be still
and know.

Suggestions

In this exercise, impressions coming from the outer and inner world are valued as equal and the purpose is to encompass both worlds as well as to find a point of silence within. The impressions coming in, via the senses and the impressions coming up from one's own mind, are observed, but not thought about or interpreted. There is a realisation of 'I am', in the midst of the world of impressions. There is no identification with any impression. Our senses, our mind and our emotions are our instruments to express our Self, our divinity. We can learn to master and use these instruments constructively. However, so often in life we are being possessed by our senses, thoughts and emotions. This exercise helps us to become silent in the middle of the world of impressions and to realise who we truly are.

25

Mindfulness III

Meditation in Action
Do what you are doing.
Be silent inside
and know
you are a part
of reality as-it-is.
Embrace with your awareness
that which you are doing.
Be aware of
every sensation,
every movement,
every change.
Embrace it.
Be one with it.
Experience unity
in multiplicity.
Immobility
in movement.
Stillness
in action.

Suggestions

Once you can remain still in the middle of impressions, you can apply this into action; for example, to remain silent and aware of the Self while walking. In Buddhist monasteries, this is practised as a walking meditation, walking in silence, slowly and very attentively. The more stimuli there are and the more complicated the action, the more difficult it will be to maintain mindfulness. A walk has a meditative component in itself and there are more activities like that. All activities in nature are very suitable, as nature bears an intrinsic silence. The Self is manifesting everywhere. But what about washing up the dishes while being mindful? Cleaning the toilet? Paying your bills? Doing the weekend shopping? Finally, the purpose of this meditation is to live mindfully in all daily hassles. Then one comes to samyama, where concentration, meditation and contemplation come together. In classical yoga philosophy, this is called karma yoga: yoga of action. Finally, meditation is not a means of withdrawing from life, but to live life to the fullest. Meditation is only meaningful when the fruits become visible in daily life; otherwise, it is a flight from reality.

III

Imaginations, Reflection, Creative Imagination and Meditation

The following chapter contains a few meditations, but mostly reflective and imaginative exercises, which are not all meditations in the strict sense of the word, according to the definition and explanation of Patanjali. These are exercises where attention is drawn inward, but now with the intention of becoming aware of yourself with a small 's'. These exercises are in service of personality work. This is the experiential path. The purpose is to be aware of yourself – your personal self – as well as your transpersonal Self, and to integrate this awareness into daily life. In these exercises, attention is not necessarily focussed single-pointedly and creative imagination is consciously used. You are being invited to use your own creative ability to give shape to your inner life as you choose.

The exercises presented in the sequence 'Reflection on the Day' are designed to help you to become aware of your actions, thoughts and emotions, and of the freedom of choice you have to change your patterns, if you like. These exercises are also suitable to train your concentration. 'Imagination' and 'Creative Imagination' are directed to playing with imagination. 'Meditation upon a Question' is a technique of problem solving involving the inner knowing. 'Meditation upon the Will' and 'Meditation upon Intention' let you become aware of the nature and use of the will and the intention. And the exercises 'Recreation of...' are several applications into practice.

The two 'Intimacy' exercises are specific meditative exercises aimed at the experience and deepening of intimacy to do with your partner.

'Meditation for Another', 'Meditation for a Group' and 'Meditation for the Earth' go beyond a personal aim.

26

Reflection on the Day I

Action
Sit down and relax.
Close your eyes.
Go in your thoughts
to the moment you woke up this morning.
See yourself lying in bed
and see yourself in course of the day
from moment to moment
doing what you did.
Watch it like an objective observer
as if you are watching a film.
Do not judge.
Do not give words to it.
Accept it as it is.
Until the moment
you sat down here.
Come back in the here and now.
Direct your attention to your body.
Breathe quietly and deeply
and stretch out.

Suggestions
This is a reflection exercise, which is very suitable as a starter. It concerns an evaluation of action. The exercise only needs to take about ten to fifteen minutes. The value of the exercise is training of concentration and visualisation ability, as well as practicing self-evaluation, and, above all, self-acceptance: watching yourself objectively, without any judgment.

27

Reflection on the Day II

Emotion
Sit down and relax.
Close your eyes.
Go in your thoughts
to the moment you woke up this morning.
See yourself lying in bed
and see yourself in course of the day
from moment to moment
feeling how you felt.
Experience your emotions once more
yet with a little distance.
Watch it like an objective observer
as if you are watching a film.
Do not judge.
Do not give words to it.
Accept it as it is
until the moment
you sat down here.
Come back in the here and now.
Direct your attention to your body.
Breathe quietly and deeply
and stretch out.

Suggestions

In this exercise you go a step further and evaluate your emotions, as you have felt throughout the day. By taking some distance from it and watching it like an observer, painful emotions will be put into perspective and lose their grip. There will be another perspective, through which space will be created to deal with emotions in another way.

28

Reflection on the Day III

Thought
Sit down and relax.
Close your eyes
Go in your thoughts
to the moment you woke up this morning.
See yourself lying in bed
and see yourself in course of the day
from moment to moment
and follow your thoughts, as you thought today.
Watch your thoughts like an objective observer
as if you are watching a film.
Do not judge.
Do not give words to it.
Accept it as it is
Until the moment
you sat down here.
Come back in the here and now.
Direct your attention to your body.
Breathe quietly and deeply
and stretch out.

Suggestions

This exercise goes another step further and you can evaluate your thoughts. It is more difficult to observe your thoughts, as if you are watching a film, without judging. When you are just observing, it will give you insight in your thought patterns. You may see correlations between your thoughts, your emotions and your actions. You may also see connections with reactions and events in your environment. Non-judgment is essential. Through this, there is a possibility of freeing yourself from burdening thought patterns by obtaining insight in these patterns and cultivating the ability of discernment.

29

Reflection on the Day IV

Recreation
Sit down and relax.
Close your eyes.
Go in your thoughts
to the moment you woke up this morning.
See yourself lying in bed
and see yourself in course of the day
from moment to moment.
Experience your actions, feelings and thoughts
as you have experienced them today.
Watch it like an objective observer
as if you are watching a film.
Do not judge.
Accept it as it is.
But do give words to it.
Is this how you would like it to be?
Is this an expression of your Self?
Or would you choose to think, feel and act differently
in a certain situation?
Produce the situation once more
And experience it anew
with a new way
of thinking, feeling and acting
on your side
until the moment you sat down here.
Come back in the here and now.
Direct your attention to your body.
Breathe quietly and deeply
and stretch out.

Suggestions

Once more, you are asked not to judge your thoughts, feelings and actions. However, this time, you are asked to give words to them. There is an essential difference between judging ('this is bad', 'I did this wrong', etc.) and verbalising. A judgement implies a rejection; verbalising something implies bringing it into the open, making it a subject of discussion. The latter is what is meant here. Name what you observe, what you experience, without judging it as good or bad. And then wonder whether this is as you would like it to be. Is this an expression of your Self, your deepest core? The choice to be who you are is yours. It is your freedom to choose.

To practice this freedom of choice you are invited in this exercise to produce certain situations anew, to recreate and to experience different thoughts, emotions and actions. By choosing your thoughts, feelings and actions anew in retrospect – and you can do this every day – you are creating a new pattern, which will gradually become manifest in your daily life. The next exercise will help you in this.

30

Reflection on the Day V

Creation
Sit down and relax.
Close your eyes.
Go in your thoughts
to the moment you shall wake up tomorrow.
See yourself lying in bed
and see yourself in course of the coming day
from moment to moment
and experience your actions, feelings and thoughts
as you may experience tomorrow.
Watch it like an objective observer
as if you are watching a film.
Do not judge.
Have no fear whether it will be like this or not.
Show how you would like it to be.
Produce the situation.
Create a way
of thinking, feeling and acting.
Make a choice about
how you want to be, think, feel and act
until the moment
you will sit down
to evaluate the day.
Come back in the here and now.
Direct your attention to your body.
Breathe quietly and deeply
and stretch out

Suggestions

This imagination exercise can be done in the morning, or in the evening, as a preparation for the coming day. You create a new pattern of how you choose to be, think, feel and act. Whether the day will really be like this is not of any relevance; you cannot control life itself; unforeseen events may happen and other circumstances may evolve. What is relevant is how you act and react, how you are living your life. Events are what they are, but you determine how you experience them. And you can realise this every day anew, every moment you can make a new choice.

When you do this exercise preceding a new day, and the Evaluation of the Day IV at the end of the day, you will not only obtain insight in your patterns, but also be able to change. You will notice that you will experience more fulfilment in your days.

This exercise is also useful to prepare for a difficult event you anticipate: an important talk, a task to be accomplished, etc.

31

Imagination I

The Place

Close your eyes

Allow the breath to become quiet.

Relax your body.

Imagine a rainbow appearing in front of you.

Slowly you step through the colours.

First you step into the colour red.

Feel how the colour red surrounds and penetrates you.

Let yourself bathe in the colour red

and experience what this colour does to you.

Then you step into the colour orange...

...the colour yellow...

...green...

...blue...

...indigo...

...and violet...

In front of you appears a white light.

Step into the light and allow your being to expand.

Then you see a staircase going down.

The staircase has twenty-one steps, which you walk down slowly.

At every step, you relax more deeply.

21... 20... 19... 18... 17... 16... 15... 14... 13... 12... 11...

10... 9... 8... 7... 6... 5... 4... 3... 2... 1...

Now you are at the place where you would wish to be,

a place you know, or which you create right now.

It may be as beautiful as you can imagine

and even more beautiful.

Look around carefully.
Listen to the sounds.
Feel the place, taste it, smell it...
When it is enough
you return to the staircase
and slowly go up the twenty-one stairs.
Every step brings you closer to the here and now.
On top of the stairs the white light appears
which you enter.
And behind is the rainbow.
You step through the colours:
violet... indigo... blue... green... yellow... orange... red...
You are back in the here and now.
Feel your body and take a few deep breaths.
Know that you can always return to your place.

Suggestions

This is a fantasy exercise, with the purpose of creating an inner space where you can be yourself, where you can withdraw from mundane life into your inner life. Here you may experience silence, be in nature, experience whatever you wish. It is an exercise to let your fantasy run free.

This visualisation of the rainbow and the stairs can be used as a start of other meditations, or as an access to other dimensions.

32

Imagination II

The Dream
Close your eyes.
Allow the breath to become quiet.
Relax your body.
Imagine a rainbow appearing in front of you.
Slowly you step through the colours.
Feel how the colours surround and penetrate you.
Let yourself bathe in the colours
and experience what the colours do to you:
red... orange... yellow... green... blue... indigo... and violet...
In front of you appears a white light.
Step into the light and allow your being to expand.
Then you see a staircase going down.
The staircase has twenty-one steps, which you walk down slowly.
At every step, you relax more deeply.
21... 20... 19... 18... 17... 16... 15... 14... 13... 12... 11...
10... 9... 8... 7... 6... 5... 4... 3... 2... 1...
Now you are at the place where you would wish to be,
a place you know, or which you create right now.
It may be as beautiful as you can imagine
and even more beautiful.
You can do and do not whatever you wish:
walk, run or fly around.
You can live out all your dreams, wishes and hidden longings.
Be the main character in your own adventure.
There are no limitations

apart from what you impose on yourself.

When it is enough

you return to the staircase

and slowly go up the twenty-one stairs.

Every step brings you closer to the here and now.

On top of the stairs the white light appears

which you enter.

And behind is the rainbow.

You step through the colours:

violet... indigo... blue... green... yellow... orange... red...

You are back in the here and now.

Feel your body and take a few deep breaths.

Know that you can always return to your place.

Suggestions

Now you can use your inner space to play, to be creative, to act out all your hidden wishes.

In our society, we are not encouraged to use our fantasy freely. Even children discover at quite an early age that their rich inner world, where everything is possible, is being dismissed by their environment as being 'only fantasy'. As if that would be inferior to the reality in which we live.

In yoga philosophy, the reality in which we live is seen as a consensus reality: a collective illusion, a relative world of opposites. We can liberate ourselves from this illusion by the practice of discernment, to become aware of what is our true nature and of what is illusion (Patanjali; II, 17-25). The next step is to practice detachment from what is unreal (Patanjali: I, 15, 16). And this is where so many people in different religious and spiritual schools pass themselves; one suppresses one's longings and desires out of the longing for liberation, or, even worse, out of the fear not to go to heaven or to go to hell.

However, we cannot pass ourselves. Our dreams, longings and desires are an intrinsic part of us. By learning to know our dreams we can learn to know our selves and then learn to liberate ourselves. We can acknowledge our desires, act them out and, finally, they will disclose our deepest wishes, which will lead us to our Self.

Fantasy can be reframed; for example, by 'creative imagination', a term from psychology. In the Dutch School for Imagination this is explained as: 'the art to wield inner images.'

Imagination is one of the most influential spontaneous functions of the human psyche. Not only gives imagination an view on what animates people, it gives them a chance to influence this in an organical and creative way. (School for Imagination, 1999)

This description points out the potential and refers to a similar kind of purpose, as described in the definition of

Patanjali, as we have seen in part I: 'Yoga is the mastery of the movements of the mind' (I, 2).

33

Imagination III

The Meeting
Close your eyes.
Allow the breath to become quiet.
Relax your body.
Imagine a rainbow appearing in front of you.
Slowly you step through the colours.
Feel how the colours surround and penetrate you.
Let yourself bathe in the colours
and experience what the colours do to you:
red... orange... yellow... green... blue... indigo... and violet...
In front of you appears a white light.
Step into the light and allow your being to expand.
Then you see a staircase going down.
The staircase has twenty-one steps, which you walk down slowly.
At every step, you relax more deeply:
21... 20... 19... 18... 17... 16... 15... 14... 13... 12... 11...
10... 9... 8... 7... 6... 5... 4... 3... 2... 1...
Now you are at the place where you would wish to be,
a place you know, or which you create right now.
It may be as beautiful as you can imagine
and even more beautiful.
You arrange a meeting
with the one you long for the most.
You may be a child meeting your Self, or God, or a loved one.
You may ask questions.
or enter into a dialogue
There are no limitations

apart from what you impose on yourself.
When it is enough
you return to the staircase
and slowly go up the twenty-one stairs.
Every step brings you closer to the here and now.
On top of the stairs the white light appears
which you enter.
And behind is the rainbow.
You step through the colours:
violet... indigo... blue... green... yellow... orange... red...
You are back in the here and now.
Feel your body and take a few deep breaths.
Know that you can always return to your place.

Suggestions

This is the dream of the meeting. Here you can use the imagination of your own space to meet someone whom you would like to meet. This may be an existent person, a deceased person, or a personification of an aspect of yourself; for example, your inner child, your masculine side, your feminine side, you at a certain age; you may meet your higher Self, etc.

You may have your meeting on a bench in a beautiful garden, in a house, in nature, or whatever kind of place your wish to create.

It is an exercise, which can be used therapeutically in all variants. In this meeting you may speak out what you have wanted to say for so long, or ask what you have wanted to ask. Do not be afraid of your imagination. Let your heart speak. Mind the phrase in the previous exercise: it is about the art of wielding your inner images.

Everyone has a bit of a child in them, with childlike longings and needs, which may not have been met, either by oneself, or by the environment in which it was raised. It can be an enrichment to connect with this inner child. Everyone has a Higher Self as well, with whom you may contact and to whom you may ask questions. In this imagination, the Self may be personified; for example, as a radiant timeless version of yourself, or an old and wise man/woman. It is also possible to meet several versions of yourself simultaneously, at different ages, or in different sub-personalities.

There are numerous possibilities with imagination, which will enable you to obtain insight in your inner images and to integrate them in your personality.

Realise that your consciousness is part of universal consciousness and you have access to this. Answers, which you may receive in this exercise, may be beyond your imagination.

34

Creative Imagination I

Close your eyes.
Relax and be still.
Direct your attention
to your breathing.
Observe your breathing
in the area of your heart.
Feel the space in your heart
and direct your attention
to your inner heart.
Feel what is living in the heart of your heart.
Ask yourself the question:
What are the wishes of my heart?
Stay focussed in your heart.
Allow the question to reverberate
and let go.
Allow the answers or images
to emerge from within.
Reflect on what has come up
and give words to it.

Suggestions

Once you have created space to listen to your heart, you may engage in what you find essential in life.

This exercise is to play with this: to allow your wishes to flow freely. When you allow yourself to fantasise to your heart's content about whatever you wish, in which everything is possible, you will naturally arrive at what is essential to you. If you could satisfy all your needs, then what would you want with your life? Then the wishes will come from within, from the Self, from love. They are no reactions to expectations that others may have from us, or to painful events form the past. There are no impulses, but consistency over a long time-span. A heart-wish concerns fulfilment and life purpose and usually extends beyond your personal life. Like the ripples in water spreading out, the fulfilment of your heart-wish will reach out to the environment.

N.B. The potential fulfilment of a wish is always there. A wish is a choice for something and in the universe there is nothing which is not possible. Everything is already there. Possibilities are infinite. What you create on an inner plane will manifest. Therefore, be cautious with your inner images!

35

Creative Imagination II

Close your eyes.
Relax and become still.
Make a wish
in your thoughts
and in your heart.
Hold this wish
in your awareness
like a red line
and create from here
a future.
Ask yourself the following questions:
What will my life look like
from the perspective of my wish
after five years?
...after ten years?
...after twenty years?
...after thirty years?
Let your imagination free.
Do not hold back.
It is your creative imagination.
Let it be as beautiful
as you can imagine
and even more beautiful.
Go beyond your limitations.
Project your image in the universe
and let go.
Allow it to sink in
and give words to it.

Suggestions

As a sequel to 'Creative Imagination I', you are now invited to fill in your wish more concretely and to visualise your life from the perspective of your heart-wish; to give that which you find truly essential a place in our life.

When you are being asked to give words to it, you are asked to phrase your reflections in order to concretise. It can be helpful to write them down or to share them with someone.

Try not to think too much during the exercise; allow images to occur from within. Do not bother about details, (im)practical-ities and (im)possibilities. It is not about being realistic this time; you may be realistic later. Now it is about playing and allowing your imagination and hidden wishes to be free.

36

Creative Imagination III

Close your eyes.
Relax and become still.
Make a wish
in your thoughts
and in your heart.
Hold this wish
in your awareness
like a red line
and create from here
a future.
Ask yourself the following questions:
What will my life look like
from the perspective of my wish
after one year?
...after six months?
...after one month?
...after one week?
...today?
Let it become concrete.
Reflect
on how you can shape your life practically
to live your wishes
now

Suggestions

The process crystallises more by moving the future towards the present. The idea behind this is that the future is being created in the present and wishes and heart-wishes can be lived only in the here and now. The question is: To what extend do you express your wishes right now? To what extend do you live your life as you find essential in the core of your heart?

When you are not content with this, you may ask: What is between the fulfilment of your wishes? Which resistances do you experience and what are you doing about them? The answer is usually more subtle than what we are inclined to think in the first place. We prefer to look for resistance outside ourselves, but finally we will find them within us. The resistance we experience in the outer world is usually reflecting our inner resistance. We, human beings, have the peculiar habit to sabotage ourselves unconsciously, especially when concerned with creating fulfilment in our lives.

There is a saying by a native medicine woman (name unknown), which expresses this beautifully:

There is nothing we are so afraid of as that which we have come for, which is: to become who we truly are.

37

Meditation upon a Question

Formulate your question
or the problem you are dealing with
briefly and clearly.
Visualise it before you
and let it go.
Close your eyes.
Breathe deeply and quietly in and out.
Relax your body.
Allow your emotions to come to rest.
Allow your thoughts to become still and clear.
Expand your awareness further,
beyond the mental,
into the realm of intuition
and inner knowing –
the knowing Self.
Allow silence in.
Take the question or the problem in your awareness.
Hold it in silence.
Penetrate to the core.
See it in its essence.
Embrace it with love.
Become one with it
and let go.
Open yourself to receive an answer.
Return to the mental plane.
Reflect and give words and images to it.

Suggestions

This meditation exercise offers a way of dealing with the questions and problems that you come across. The question is taken to the realm of the higher mental or abstract thinking, which is beyond the rational mind (in Sanskrit this is called 'manas') and into the realm of buddhi, intuition and inner knowing. This means that the question is not being thought through; the question is being held in one's awareness as concisely as possible so that only its core remains.

It is important in this exercise to formulate your question as clearly as possible in advance. A question which can only be answered with 'yes' or 'no' is not advisable, because this implies that there are only two possibilities of choice, while there are numerous possibilities for any question and any problem. Keep your question open and free from presumptions. Think thoroughly about the core of your question before you enter the exercise. What is it that you really want to know? This is a contemplative process in itself. When the key question or key problem is taken to the higher mental and intuitive plane, penetrate through it; go beyond words; become one with the question. There is a saying that the answer to a question is hidden within the problem. The question, however, also hides the solution to that problem. Let go of your question; surrender to a consciousness more expanded than your own. Open yourself to receive an answer. Sometimes, this may take some time and the answer is revealed to you throughout the following days. It may be a sign, a symbol your eye catches, or a phrase suddenly popping up in your mind. You will recognise it and know.

When you come out of the exercise, take time to reflect and phrase your experience; write it down and stay alert to further inspirations.

38

Meditation upon the Will

Close your eyes.
Breathe deeply and quietly, in and out.
Relax your body.
Allow your emotions to come to rest.
Allow your thoughts to become still and clear.
Direct you attention to the will
(your own personal will).
Feel your will as a power
flowing through you.
Feel how your will shapes your thoughts,
colours your emotions,
governs your actions.
Sense the quality of your will:
Is it flexible or headstrong?
...clear or obscure?
...loving or cold?
...or...?
How do you use your will in your life?
Direct your attention to the Self
(your transpersonal Self)
and feel the will
at the level of the Self.
Sense the quality of the will of the Self:
Let your personal will become transparent
so that it reflects the will of the Self.
Sense the power of the will of the Self
flowing through you,
shaping your thoughts,

colouring your emotions,

governing your actions.

Visualise yourself manifesting the will of the Self.

Suggestions

The purpose of this exercise is to experience the difference between the nature of the personal will and of the transpersonal will. The will is a power (it is no coincidence that see speak of 'willpower'). Often, we are influenced unconsciously by our will, our own personal will. It shapes our thoughts, colours our emotions and governs our actions. We want without knowing.

A first step is to become aware of our will, and how we use it and next to attune to our transpersonal will of the Self.

The will of the Self is called 'intention' in the following exercise.

39

Meditation upon Intention

Close your eyes.
Breathe deeply and quietly, in and out.
Relax your body.
Allow your emotions to come to rest.
Allow your thoughts to become still and clear.
Ask yourself the question:
What do I want?
What is my intention?*
Reflect upon this
and then let go.
Make yourself receptive
for an answer from the Self.
Allow the answer to sink in your awareness
without judgement.
Formulate now the intention you have
(briefly and clearly).
Hold this as a seed-thought in your awareness.
Let this intention shape your thoughts
and govern your words and actions.

Suggestions

*Intention is the will and aspiration of the Self to manifest; it is not a desire of the personal 'I'. It is an individual purpose, in service of a higher vision. You may ask the question concerning the intention you have in your life, in your work, your relationship, or in your meditation practice. It is the intention at this moment which counts – your sincere intention. Each intention is legitimate. Whether your intention is directed towards yourself (to be happy, to learn, to grow), or directed towards the benefit of others, it is okay. Personal growth is always for the benefit of a wider context.

It may be necessary first to play and to fulfil all kinds of needs and desires – to act out fantasies, to make a lot of fun – before any intention of the Self can be sensed. And that is okay. To play, to fantasise and to create is wonderful and this will not stop once one connects with the Self; on the contrary, I would say! The Self is very playful and joyful.

The art is to accept who you are. You are fine the way you are. Would you like to be different? Would you like to grow? The choice is yours.

This meditation is designed to find out about your deeper needs, wishes and intentions. You may go further and ask yourself what intention exists behind your intention.

40

Recreation of Yourself

Close your eyes.
Breathe deeply and quietly, in and out.
Relax your body.
Allow your emotions to come to rest.
Allow your thoughts to become still and clear.
Ask yourself the question:
Who do I like to Be?
Who do I like to Be? – physically
                       – emotionally
                       – mentally
                       – as Self
This is your truth, your reality,
your intention.
Let go of all thoughts, emotions and actions
which fail the reality you choose now.
Align your thoughts, feelings and actions
to your image of Self.
Visualise this reality in all its glory.
Give it an emotional charge – a wish.
Create this reality
here and now.
Project the image in the universe
and let go.

Suggestions

We often ask our children: 'What do you want to become later?'

We refer to a profession or a role in society, but some children just answer: 'Me.' This is what is meant here:

Who do you like to be?

Who: It is about who you would like to be, as a human being. It is not about what you want to show the world in a certain role.

Do: This implies some kind of activity. There is something needed from your side. You are being asked to like, to intend.

You: You, YOU as a person, as an individual, with your unique qualities.

Like: This implies a choice, freedom to shape yourself and your life as you wish, according to your intention.

To Be: It is about being, not about doing.

We create with our thoughts, emotions and actions. When we align all of these with our vision, we shall be who we like to be. From here we shall do what we like to do.

41

Recreation of Qualities

Take in your mind
a quality-to-develop*
and let go.
Close your eyes.
Breathe deeply and quietly, in and out.
Relax your body.
Allow your emotions to come to rest.
Allow your thoughts to become still and clear.
Expand your awareness
beyond the mental,
into the realm of the intuition
and inner knowing –
the wisdom of the Self.
Realise that you are the Self.
Take the quality-to-develop
in your awareness
and let it be.
Accept it.
Get to know it.
Look at its essence.
Embrace it with love.
Visualise the potential of this quality
in transformed form.
Visualise this quality
manifesting in a constructive way in your life.
Visualise how you may express this quality
in your words and actions
and integrate it in your being.

Suggestions

*The term 'quality-to-develop' is a neutral description of a shadow side, weak side or negative quality. Its title is self-explanatory – 'quality-to-develop' – a quality in potential, which needs to be developed. In the present stage, this quality is being expressed negatively. Shadow sides are often ignored, suppressed or hidden, to come out with full force when we are emotionally hit, wiped off our feet, etc. Shadow sides, however, are sun sides in potential, but they need to be acknowledged, accepted and integrated. This exercise is designed to help us recognise and acknowledge our qualities-to-be on order to be able to use them, instead of letting them use us.

42

Recreation of Fear

Formulate in your mind
a fear – something you are afraid of
and let go.
Close your eyes.
Breathe deeply and quietly, in and out.
Relax your body.
Allow your emotions to come to rest.
Allow your thoughts to become still and clear.
Expand your awareness
beyond the mental,
into the realm of the intuition
and inner knowing –
the transpersonal Self.
This is who you truly are.
The Self knows no fear.
The Self is free.
Look straight at your fear
from the perspective of the Self
and ask yourself the question:
Is this a realistic fear?
Does this fear concern a present reality as it is?
When it does not,
ask yourself the question:
Can I change this fear?
Do I want to change it?
Open yourself up to a new reality –
the reality of the Self.
Choose another thought.

Choose another reality
free from fear.
Visualise this reality.
Let it become true in your imagination.
Imagine that you think, feel and act accordingly.

Suggestions

According to Patanjali, fear is one of the five causes of all suffering (II, 2-10).

Primarily, there is *lack of awareness of reality*, to hold the non-self for the Self. From here *egoism* develops; we think that we are this 'I', and from this separated 'I' we get *attracted* to certain matters and *repulsed* by other matters. From here, *fear* develops: fear to lose the 'I', to lose ourselves, of dying, fear of pain, fear of the unknown, fear to lose something or someone we feel attached to, or fear of what might happen to us, fear of failure, fear of loneliness, etc.

So, actually misery is based upon lack of awareness of reality. Most fears are unrealistic; they do not concern the present reality, but the future or the past, so they are illusionary.

One suffers the most from the suffering he fears, which will never happen.

Patanjali says, however:

The misery which is not yet come can and is to be avoided (II, 16).

He continues to explain that causes of misery can be avoided by the realisation of who we truly are (II, 17).

Therefore, in this exercise, we direct our awareness to the transpersonal Self.

When we realise that we are the Self, there is no fear. At the level of the Self, there is no separation, but oneness, love and discernment. We use this discernment to negate the fear. Finally, fear is replaced by a constructive thought, which serves us better.

43

Recreation of Thought

Take a thought in your mind
which bothers you.
Reflect upon it for a while
and let go.
Close your eyes.
Breathe deeply and quietly, in and out.
Relax your body.
Allow your emotions to come to rest.
Allow your thoughts to become still and clear.
Ask yourself the following questions:
Is this a real thought?
Is this thought according to my truth?
Does this thought serve my purpose?
If this is not the case
then ask yourself:
Can I change this?
Am I willing to change this?
Look at your thought from another perspective.
Open up to a new reality.
Be prepared to go beyond your imagination.
Choose a new thought
which is in accordance with your truth
and which serves you.
Visualise this.
Give new words to it.

Suggestions

This exercise is a meditative variant of a well known exercise in psychology, the RET (Rational Emotive Therapy), and in the NLP (Neuro-Linguistic Programming). The thought behind this exercise is classically philosophical and Buddhist:

Reality is as it is, but our thoughts about it determine how we experience reality.

The challenge of this exercise is to explore a thought or situation which bothers you, as objectively as you can, and investigate whether this thought is based on reality. It requires some practise to learn to distinguish which thoughts are real and which are not. It is helpful to imagine how a hidden camera would record the situation. We may also wonder whether the thought is desirable or not. Does it lead to desirable feelings, results or interactions?

Some recurrent unrealistic thoughts are:

'...Have to...': We often think that we 'have to', but, at closer examination, this mostly means that we may or may not want to. 'Usually, we have to...': And often by ourselves, because we think that, otherwise, the world will collapse, or others might think badly of us that, or we won't be good enough, or we won't deserve to... whatever.

But what will happen when you won't do it?

The relevant question is: What do you really want?

Many thoughts that are unrealistic are thoughts of self-judgement, self-doubt or expectations that others might judge us. The relevant question is: Who do you like to be?

When the thought is clarified, the art is to reframe and rephrase this thought into a new one and to act and feel accordingly.

44

Recreation of Relationships I

Love
Take in your mind a person
with whom you want to share your love.
Visualise him/her clearly
and let go of the image.
Close your eyes.
Breathe deeply and quietly, in and out.
Relax your body.
Allow your emotions to come to rest.
Allow your thoughts to become still and clear.
Expand your awareness
beyond the mental.
Direct your attention to the Self.
Sense the love and wisdom of the Self.
Be in silence.
Take the image of your person in your awareness.
Visualise this person clearly.
What connects the two of you?
Where do you feel this connection?
Connect consciously from heart to heart.
See the other as Self,
radiant and multi-dimensional*
and see the other as a personality
with all his/her possibilities and limitations.
Allow the other to be as he/she is
without wanting to change him/her.
Embrace him/her with your love.
Let your love be nurturing

and let go of the other.
Let him/her be free.
Direct your attention to your body.
Take a few deep breaths
and come back in the here and now.

Suggestions

This exercise can be applied to consciously experience and nurture the relationship with people you love. It may also serve to support people in times of illness or difficulty, as a more subtle variant of 'I think of you!' The exercise works according to basic principles of healing. It is very important not to want to impose anything on the other (not even your love), but to see the other as an individual Self; allow him/her his/her own dignity.

*We are all multidimensional beings; We each have a physical body and a personality with unique oddities and short-comings. Beyond that, we are soul and Self, and finally a part of universal consciousness. It is an art to see the Self within yourself as well as within the other, to see beyond personal traits, possibilities and limitations. When you can perceive a human being throughout the different dimensions, you can do nothing other than love them. Principally, he/she is not separated from you. By seeing the Self within the other, you are giving a gift and the possibility for him/her to experience him/herself in this expanded perspective.

45

Recreation of Relationships II

Forgiveness
Take in your mind a person
for whom you hold negative feelings.*
Visualise him/her clearly
and let go of the image.
Close your eyes.
Breathe deeply and quietly, in and out.
Relax your body.
Allow your emotions to come to rest.
Allow your thoughts to become still and clear.
Expand your awareness
beyond the mental.
Direct your attention to the Self.
Sense the love and wisdom of the Self.
Be in silence.
Take the image of your person in your awareness.
Visualise this person clearly.
What connects the two of you?
Where do you feel this connection?
Connect consciously from heart to heart.
See the other as Self,
radiant and multi-dimensional*
and see the other as a personality
with all his/her possibilities and limitations.
Allow the other to be as he/she is
without wanting to change him/her.
Offer him/her your apologises
for what you have done to him/her.

Speak out this apology.
Forgive him/her what he/she has done to you.
Speak out this forgiveness.
Embrace him/her with your love
and let go of the other.
Direct your attention to your body.
Take a few deep breaths
and come back in the here and now.

Suggestions

* This may be someone who has done something to you, or someone to whom you have done something.

This exercise is complementary to the previous one. It is easier to connect with love from heart to heart and to see someone as Self when there is a bond of affection. It is a real challenge to connect this way when one experiences tension, irritation, aversion, anger or indifference. This exercise has a healing affect on relationships. Even though there is no actual interaction, even when the other is a deceased person, something is healed.

This can be explained as followed:

When two (or more) people are connected (in friendship or in animosity; in a family or at work; in an intimate relationship or just a superficial acquaintance), an energetic exchange is taking place and an energetic bond is formed. The more intensive and intimate the relationship, the stronger the bond. These bonds may survive time and space, life and death. When there are painful thoughts and feelings between the two, the bond gets disturbed, which influences both parties. An exercise like this heals the disturbance from one side. Although the other need not be aware of this, at least one of the two has different feelings and behaviour, which naturally influences both parties. Realise that disturbances in a relationship are always a part of the reality of both parties. However, each has the capacity and also the responsibility to change his own image of his reality. It is not about guilt or judgement; it is about taking responsibility for your side of the story.

It is always preferable to speak to the person concerned to solve the conflict, but this meditation may be used as a preparation or a supplement to this.

46

Intimacy I

Sit down with your partner
facing each other,
as close as possible
without touching each other.
Close your eyes.
Breathe deeply and quietly, in and out.
Relax your body.
Allow your emotions and thoughts to come to rest.
Find the silence within.
Align with your Self.
Experience yourself as Self.
Open yourself to the other
so that he/she may see your Self
and open yourself to perceive the Self in the other.
When you are ready
stretch out your hands to the other
and touch
(the eyes remain closed).
Feel the other through his/her hands.
Receive the other; give to the other.
Be aware of the stream of giving and receiving.
When you are ready
let go of the hands.
Open your eyes.
Look at each other.
Look into each other's eyes.
See the Self.
Be aware of the stream of giving and receiving.

When it is enough, or too much, you close your eyes
and go back into yourself
until you can open up again.
Close your eyes.
Let go of each other.
Give each other space.
Experience your own space,
your own strength.
Relax.

Suggestions

This exercise can be done with anybody: a life partner, a friend or a stranger. It is a suitable exercise to do within groups, to deepen connections and trust. It is about intimacy in its pure meaning.

To what extend are you showing yourself (your Self) and to what extend are you prepared to see the other?

How far do you let the other in and how far do you dare to be in the other?

Once you have looked someone into the eyes this way, this person will never be the same to you.

47

Intimacy II

Sexuality
Sit down with your partner
facing each other,
as close as possible
without touching each other.
Close your eyes.
Breathe deeply and quietly, in and out.
Relax your body.
Allow your emotions and thoughts to come to rest.
Find the silence within.
Align with your Self.
Experience yourself as Self.
Open yourself to the other
so that he/she may see your Self
and open yourself to see the Self in the other.
Open the eyes and look at each other.
Look into each other's eyes.
See the Self.
Look at each other from head to toe
and allow yourself to be looked at.
Let the looking be as a touch.
Be aware of the other.
Be aware of your sensuality
and be aware of the Self.
When it is enough, or too much, you close your eyes
and go back into yourself
until you can open up again.
Touch the other

slowly and consciously
of Self and sensuality.
The other is still and receives.
Alternate giving and receiving
until you are touching each other
and giving and receiving
simultaneously,
being self and the other.
One in Self.

Suggestions

This is an extension of intimacy as foreplay and a deepening of
sex. There are numerous variants to be imagined. The underlying
thought is found in Tantra. Tantra is an old tradition, which aims
at spiritual union amongst other things by means of sexuality.
Sexuality is used (and sometimes abused) to come to self-realisation by surrender and by seeing the universal Self in the other.
This may happen when there is communication and merging at a
physical, emotional, mental level and at the level of the Self. The
interaction is not intended to lead to an orgasm, but to invoke a
mutual ecstasy with and within each other. The partner is seen, as
well as man/woman, as a soul, as Higher Self, as a cosmic lover,
as God/Goddess.

48

Meditation for Another

Choose someone to whom you want to dedicate this meditation and be aware of why.

Formulate a wish for the other.*

Close your eyes.
Breathe deeply and quietly, in and out.
Relax your body.
Allow your emotions to come to rest.
Allow your thoughts to become still and clear.
Expand your awareness
beyond the mental.
Direct your attention to the Self.
Be in silence.
Take your wish for the other in your awareness.
Hold this wish in your heart.
Clothe your wish with love
(all love there is inside of you)
and let go of the wish.
Let go of the other.
Direct your attention to your body.
Breathe in and out quietly
and come back in the here and now.

Suggestions

*A wish for another should only arise from love, in which the other is accepted completely as he/she is. By no means is the integrity of another to be affected. It is not manipulation; it is not a wish for yourself that the other would become as you wish. It is a dedication of the qualities of your Self to the other. In other words: to use the love of the Self, your Self, for the benefit of another.

In order to avoid any kind of interference with egocentric interest, the best thing is to keep your wish universal, like wishing someone love, good health, strength, joy or another quality of the Self. Another possibility is to have the other person's permission for a concrete wish, which can be discussed and meditated upon by both parties.

To dedicate a meditation to another, if unconditionally and selflessly, is a powerful and fruitful method of meditation. It is a similar principle to praying for someone.

49

Meditation for a Group

Sit as a group in a circle.
Discuss a collective intention, a wish or a seed-thought
which may serve as topic for the meditation.
Close your eyes.
Breathe deeply and quietly, in and out.
Relax your body.
Allow your emotions to come to rest.
Allow your thoughts to become still and clear.
Expand your awareness
beyond the mental.
Direct your attention to the Self.
Be in silence.
Be aware of the group.
Visualise the other members in your mind.
Connect with each other from heart to heart.
Go beyond all personal differences.
See each member of the group as a transpersonal Self.
Connect with each other at the level of the Self.
Join the collective attention
and direct this at the seed-thought.
Hold the seed-thought in collective awareness –
silence.
Then let go of the seed-thought.
Let go of the group.
Breathe in and out quietly
and come back in the here and now.

Suggestions

A seed-thought is mentioned here and, at this point, the meditation can be followed as described in the meditation, 'A Seed-thought'. However, one of the other meditations can be done as well; for example, 'Meditation upon the Intention', 'Meditation for Another', or 'Meditation for the Earth'.

Basically, all meditations can be practised in a group; some can be guided verbally, others are more suitable for practice in silence.

When meditation is practised with a collective intention and in alignment with each other, the power accumulates. In this meditation, this alignment and joining is carried out consciously.

50

Meditation for the Earth

Close your eyes.
Breathe deeply and quietly, in and out.
Relax your body.
Allow your emotions to come to rest.
Allow your thoughts to become still and clear.
Expand your awareness
beyond the mental.
Direct your attention to the Self.
Be in silence
then expand your awareness
beyond your transpersonal Self,
to universal Self.
Visualise that you stretch out
and move into space.
See the Earth as a planet from the perspective of outer space
in all her beauty,
with all the life she is carrying.
See the Earth as a big living organism.
See the illness and the health
caused by mankind.
Connect with the Earth.
Let the love and strength of the Self
stream out over the Earth.
Silence.
Let go of the Earth.
Withdraw in yourself.
Breathe in and out quietly
and come back in the here and now.

Suggestions

One could think of numerous variants to this meditation. One could direct one's attention to specific problem areas on Earth: areas of war, starvation, environmental disaster or pollution.

A meditation dedicated to the Earth is not meant as a substitute for goal-directed action. It is not meant to be a solution for all problems. It is meant as a method of building your awareness and remaining alert to the necessity of the recovery and maintenance of the balance on our planet. Meditation can also inspire problem-solving thinking and the necessary action.

In addition to this, energy follows thought. It is better to direct our attention collectively, and in a constructive way, to a better liveable planet than to our personal struggles. Any change begins with a change in consciousness.

Epilogue

Meditation as a Way of Life

The meditations described in this book are only a small selection of what is possible. However, more important than variations in methods is the way in which you integrate meditation in your life. What will you take home, to your work, in your relations? How do you live your meditation?

A first aspect of meditation is to be able to reach a deep state of relaxation: physical relaxation, emotional quietness and mental silence. This is a prerequisite for entering meditation. The practice of meditation begins with the training of relaxation and to learn to withdraw within in a point of inner silence. Once you are trained in this, this is something which will naturally bear fruits in your life. This will prove most evident in situations of stress and times of hardship, when you are challenged to maintain your inner balance. Can you relax when necessary and withdraw in yourself, in the Self, to draw on your inner source? Are you able to take some objective perspective and distance from your personal self and the impressions, questions and problems brought along by the days? If so, can you make other choices if you wish? Are you able to express your creativity in your life? Can you express yourself (your Self) in your relationships? Can you allow others to be themselves – their Self?

Then there is the ability to concentrate, which will show in work, study, intensity of experience and the ability to process information.

Above all, meditation offers the possibility for transformation, to expand the perspective you have about who you are and what the world is, and to refine the quality of your life. Then, the fruits of meditation will show in the state of peace and joy in your whole way of being.

Meditation is not a guarantee for happiness. You may be

happy when your needs are fulfilled (these may be primary needs, material needs, needs in areas of career, relationships, creativity, personal development and finally self-realisation), but meditation does not provide in all these needs. It is a technique of discernment, a way of life with which you become aware of your potential, the possibilities of your mind, of your true Self, which will enable you to lead your life according to your intention. This will lead to life joy: not the pleasure which you feel when you get what you want or when things go as you like, but the joy which springs from within because you live life to the fullest. Life will not change, your attitude towards life will change and, consequently, you will be able to transform your life.

References

Most principles in this book are based on the Yoga Sutras of Patanjali, of which I have used the following version:

Taimni, I. K., *The Science of Yoga: A Commentary on the Yoga-Sutras of Patanjali in the Light of Modern Thought*. Madras: Theosophical Publishing House, 1961.

B.K.S. Iyengar, *Light on the Yoga Sutras of Patanjali*. London: Thorsons, 1993.

B.K.S. Iyengar, *Light On Life*. Emmaus, USA, 2005

School voor Imaginatie, Programma 1999-2000, Ruysdaelkade 29, 1072AH Amsterdam.

(This list is not complete yet, I'd like to do this in accordance with the publisher)

BOOKS

6th Books investigates the paranormal,
supernatural, explainable or unexplainable.
Titles cover everything included within
parapsychology: how to, lifestyles, beliefs,
myths, theories and memoir.